Monkey Colors

Darrin Lunde
Illustrated by **Patricia J. Wynne**

ini Charlesbridge

Monkeys come in many colors.

woolly spider monkey

Some monkeys are yellow,

red howler monkey

and some are red.

Japanese macaque

Some are brown,

golden lion tamarin

and some are orange.

Monkeys come in many colors.

mandrill

This monkey has a blue and red nose,

Yunnan snub-nosed monkey

and this monkey has pink lips.

black and white colobus monkey

This monkey is black
and white,

and these monkeys have orange feet.

Monkeys come in many colors.

Some monkeys are orange
when young

silvered langurs

and gray when old.

Other monkeys are gold if girls

black and gold howler monkeys

and black if boys.

Another kind of monkey
has an orange face,
white lips, orange ears,
black shoulders, white arms,
and black and red legs.

red-shanked douc langur

Monkeys come in many colors.

Which monkey is your favorite?

The **woolly spider monkey** uses its long arms, legs, and tail to swing through the trees. It is an endangered species.

Red howler monkeys give a loud roaring call that can be heard over long distances in the rain forest.

Japanese macaques are good swimmers and love to soak in hot springs near volcanoes.

The **golden lion tamarin** gets its name from the thick mane of orange fur around its face. These endangered monkeys were once more common in zoos than in the wild. Today scientists are trying to return more of them to the wild.

Mandrills use their brightly colored faces to show who is in charge. The animal with the most colorful face is usually the leader of the group.

The **Yunnan snub-nosed monkey** lives in just one small area in the snowy mountains of southwest China. It is an endangered species.

Black and white colobus monkeys live in the highest treetops. They can find fresh young leaves there, but they have to watch out for eagles swooping down from above.

Midas tamarins get their name from the legend of King Midas. Anything he touched turned to gold. Can you see why this monkey is named after Midas?

Infant **silvered langurs** are born bright orange and look very different from the gray-colored adults. Their orange fur turns gray when they are a few months old.

Male **black and gold howler monkeys** are almost twice as heavy as females. The males are always black, and the females are always golden yellow in color.

The **moustached monkey** is one of many different kinds of guenon monkeys living in tropical Africa. When different species of guenon travel together, they use their colorful markings to tell each other apart.

When an endangered **red-shanked douc langur** wants to play, it closes its eyes to show its pale blue eyelids. This is called a "play face."

Europe

Asia

Africa

Indian Ocean

Australia

red-shanked douc langur

Japanese macaque

Yunnan snub-nosed monkey

silvered langur

black and white colobus monkey

Monkeys are primates.

All primates have big brains and highly movable fingers. Not all primates are monkeys. Some examples of primates that are not monkeys are the lemurs of Madagascar, the galagos of Africa, the tarsiers of Asia, and all the apes. Apes include gorillas, orangutans, chimpanzees, bonobos, and gibbons—as well as us humans.

For Saki.—D. L.

For all young artists. Keep drawing!—P. J. W.

Author's Note

The monkeys in this book would never be seen together in the wild or in a zoo. The only place where you can see all these monkeys together and up close is in a natural history museum. Museums are some of the best places to study the great diversity of animals on Earth. If you can, plan to visit a natural history museum near you.

Published by Charlesbridge
85 Main Street
Watertown, MA 02472
(617) 926-0329
www.charlesbridge.com

Library of Congress Cataloging-in-Publication Data
Lunde, Darrin P.
    Monkey colors / Darrin Lunde ; illustrated by Patricia J. Wynne.
        p. cm.
    ISBN 978-1-57091-741-7 (reinforced for library use)
    ISBN 978-1-57091-742-4 (softcover)
1. Monkeys—Color—Juvenile literature. I. Wynne, Patricia, ill. II. Title.
QL737.P9L86 2011
599.8—dc22   2011000669

Printed in China
(hc) 10 9 8 7 6 5 4 3 2 1
(sc) 10 9 8 7 6 5 4 3 2 1

Illustrations done in watercolor and ink on Arches hot-press watercolor paper
Display type and text type set in Mister Earl, Franklin Gothic, and Felt Tip
Color separations by KHL Chroma Graphics, Singapore
Printed and bound February 2012 by Jade Productions in Heyuan,
    Guangdong, China
Production supervision by Brian G. Walker
Designed by Martha MacLeod Sikkema